Table of Contents

Genealogical Research in Alabama

Alabama has, since its beginning, been a seat of cultural diversity; as such it is rich in genealogical materials. The earliest settlers were of course Native Americans, while the first Europeans arrived in the state in the mid-16th century. There are and abundance of genealogical records available for Alabama, especially from the 18th and 19th centuries due to the rush of settlers who flocked there during the "Alabama Fever" period in the early 1800's. This page is dedicated to those records and helping you to understand:

1.   What they are
2.   Where to find them
3.   How to use them

These valuable resources can be found both online and off, so we'll introduce you to some online databases and indexes, as well as the many brick-and-mortar repositories, societies and organizations that will help with your genealogical research in Alabama.

In order to give you a more comprehensive understanding of these records, a brief history of the "Yellowhammer State" is provided in order to help you understand what kind of records may have been generated in a particular area during a particular time period. That information will further help you to pinpoint times and locations on which to focus your research.

A Brief History of Alabama

The earliest inhabitants of Alabama were Native Americans, mainly of the Tawasa and Pawokti tribes. The Spaniards arrived in 1540 under the charge of Hernando De Soto. The Spaniards left fairly quickly after finding no gold there, but they left behind diseases which rapidly reduced the Native American population. The next Europeans to arrive were the French, who established the first major settlement in the late 17th century.

The French were not popular with the Native Americans who favored the superior quality products of the British traders, and subsequently a series of wars were fought between the French and British for control of the region. The British finally gained control of the area after the culmination of the French Indian War (1754-1763), which saw the British soundly defeating the French. The British controlled the area until after the Revolutionary war, after which Alabama was ceded to the United States of America.

Important Genealogical Dates in Alabama History

1702 – Mobile (first settlement) founded by the French.

1763 – Ceded by France to the British.

1783 – West Florida part of Alabama ceded from Great Britain to Spain.

1798 – Alabama ceded to the United States and forms part of the Mississippi Territory

1805 - Indian cessions opened up to white settlement. This included large portions of western (Choctaw) and northern (Chickasaw and Cherokee) Alabama.

1811– 812 – First schools, Washington Academy and Green Academy) established.

1817 – Organized as separate U.S. territory.

1819 – Statehood

1820 – First Federal census of Alabama

1832 – First railroad opened.

1836-1837 – Indians driven from their homelands in Second Creek War

1849 – Capitol Montgomery destroyed by fire.

1861 – Secedes from the Union

1868 – Readmitted to Union

Famous Battles Fought in Alabama

Below you will find a list of links to websites containing information on famous battles fought in Alabama. They can provide regimental and other historical data that can help you to locate military records for ancestors.

Battle of Athens http://patriotpost.us/alexander/13407

Battle of Day's Gap
http://americancivilwar.50megs.com/DaysGap.html

Battle of Decatur
http://www.civilwaralbum.com/misc17/decatur1.htm

Battle of Fort Blakely http://www.civilwar.org/battlefields/fort-blakely.html

Battle of Mobile Bay http://www.civilwar.org/battlefields/mobile-bay.html

Battle of Newton
http://www.exploresouthernhistory.com/newtonbattle.html

Battle of Selma
http://www.exploresouthernhistory.com/selmabattle.html

Battle of Spanish Fort
http://www.exploresouthernhistory.com/spanishfort.html

Common Alabama Genealogical Issues and Resources to Overcome Them

Boundary Changes: A major issue in researching Alabama ancestors are historical boundary changes. It is common to be searching for an ancestor's record in one county when in fact it is stored in a different one due to county boundaries being changed. The **Atlas of Historical County Boundaries** can help you to overcome that problem. It provides a chronological listing of every boundary change that has occurred in the history of Alabama.

Atlas of Historical County Boundaries
http://publications.newberry.org/ahcbp/pages/Alabama.html

Name Changes: Surname changes, variations, and misspellings can complicate genealogical research. It is important to check all spelling variations. Soundex, a program that indexes names by sound, is a useful first step, but you can't rely on it completely as some name variations result in different Soundex codes. The surnames could be different, but the first name may be different too. You can also find records filed under initials, middle names, and nicknames as well, so you will need to check spellings in order to cover all the possibilities.

Alabama Genealogical Organizations and Archives

Genealogical resources include not only records, but the organizations that house them, or can direct you to them. These institutions include: *Archives, Libraries, Genealogical Societies, Family History Centers, Universities, Churches, and Museums.*

Following are links to their websites, their physical addresses, and a summary of the records you can find there.

Archives

Alabama State Archives (Department of Archives and History) – Local and county governmental records, church and synagogue records, Civil War records, 1867 Voter Registration database, military records, city directories, land records, maps, historical newspapers.

P.O. Box 300100 / 624
Washington Ave.
Montgomery, AL 36130
Tel: (334) 242-4435
Email: mark.palmer@archives.alabama.gov

Website: http://www.archives.alabama.gov/

Auburn University Libraries – Agricultural records, historical photographs, church records, family histories, institutional records, agricultural records, Civil War records, manuscripts, rare books, and selected artifacts.

231 Mell Street
Auburn, Alabama 36849
Tel: (334) 844-4500 or (800) 446-0387
EMail: libwebm@auburn.edu

Website: http://www.lib.auburn.edu/specialcollections//

University of South Alabama Archives – Civil War records, manuscripts, birth records, death records, divorce records, marriage records, naturalization records, orphan records, passenger lists, burial records, wills, land records.

1504 Springhill Avenue
Room 0722,
Mobile AL 36604
Tel: 251.434.3800
Fax: 251.434.3622
EMail: mccalllib@southalabama.edu

Website: http://www.southalabama.edu/archives/

Alabama Bureau of Vital Statistics – birth, death, marriage, and divorce certificates, certificates of foreign birth, adoption information.

The RSA Tower
201 Monroe Street
Montgomery, AL 36104

Postal Address:

P.O. Box 303017
Montgomery, AL 36130-3017

Tel: (334) 206-5300 (8:00 a.m. - 5:00 p.m.) or
1-800-ALA-1818
EMail: On Site Contact Form

Alabama Bureau of Vital Statistics
http://www.adph.org/vitalrecords/?id=1559

Mobile Public Library – Indian Rolls, Confederate pension records, business records, family papers, Confederate rosters, probate records, census records, city directories,

Mobile Public Library
700 Government St,

Mobile AL 36602
Tel: 251-208-7073

Website: http://www.mplonline.org/local-history-and-genealogy.html#.Ujg2j9LTzdM

University of Alabama Hoole Library – manuscripts, historical maps, historical photographs, Civil War materials, slave and runaway records.

University Libraries
The University of Alabama
P.O. Box 870266
Tuscaloosa, Alabama 35487-0266

Tel: (205) 348-0500

Website: http://www.lib.ua.edu/libraries/hoole/

Alabama Genealogical and Historical Societies

Genealogical and historical societies have access to extensive catalogues of genealogical data, and offer expert guidance for genealogical research. Many members are professional genealogists who are most willing to share their expertise in finding ancestors.

Alabama Genealogical Society - Works with Samford University Library - Special Collection Department - to handle correspondence and maintain the genealogical records of the society. They house various genealogical and historical resources, which are accessible to the public and maintains a list of member-genealogists who are willing to do research for a fee.

Website: http://algensoc.org/

The Alabama Historical Association - is the oldest statewide historical society in Alabama. They sponsor *The Alabama Review*, a quarterly journal of Alabama and two Newsletters each year.

Website: http://www.archives.state.al.us/aha/aha.html

The Montgomery Genealogical Society - a non-profit corporation located in Montgomery, Alabama, they promote research into families with connections to Montgomery County.

Website: http://www.rootsweb.ancestry.com/~almgs/

Birmingham Historical Society - contains a small amount of information available to its members though annual publications and newsletters.

Website: http://www.bhistorical.org/

Tennessee Valley Historical Society – Founded in order to unite people interested in pursuing historical and genealogical research in the Muscle Shoals area of northwest Alabama, and to accumulate and preserve records and artifacts related to such.

Website: http://home.hiwaay.net/~mahan/tvhs.htm

Alabama Daughters of the Revolution – The Alabama Chapter of the DAR

Website: http://www.alabamadar.org/home.html

Sons of Confederate Veterans Alabama Division - dedicated to preserving the true history of the period 1861-1865; an excellent resource for researching Confederate Civil War ancestors.

Website: http://www.aladivscv.com/

Alabama Family History Centers

The Family History Centers run by the LDS Church offer free access to billions of genealogical records for free to the general public. They also provide classes on genealogy and one-on-one assistance to inexperienced family historians. Here you will find a **Complete Listing of Alabama Family History Centers**.

Complete Listing of Alabama Family History Centers

https://familysearch.org/locations/centerlocator

Additional Genealogical Resources

Alabama Mailing Lists

Mailing lists are internet based facilities that use email to distribute a single message to all who subscribe to it. When information on a particular surname, new records, or any other important genealogy information related to the mailing list topic becomes available, the subscribers are alerted to it. Joining a mailing list is an excellent way to stay up to date on Alabama genealogy research topics. Rootsweb have an extensive listing of **Alabama Mailing Lists** on a variety of topics.

Alabama Mailing Lists
http://lists.rootsweb.ancestry.com/index/usa/AL/misc.html

Alabama Message Boards

A message board is another internet based facility where people can post questions about a specific genealogy topic and have it answered by other genealogists. If you have questions about a surname, record type, or research topic, you can post your question and other researchers and genealogists will help you with the answer. You must make sure to check back regularly, as the answers are not emailed to you. The message boards at the **Alabama Genealogy Forum** are completely free to use.

Alabama Genealogy Forum http://genforum.genealogy.com/al/

Alabama Periodicals

Many genealogy periodicals contain reprinted copies of family genealogies, transcripts of family Bible records, information about local records and archives, census indexes, church records, queries, land records, obituaries, court records, cemetery records, and wills. These **Alabama Genealogy Periodicals** are well worth adding to your genealogical arsenal.

Alabama Genealogy Periodicals
https://familysearch.org/learn/wiki/en/Alabama_Periodicals

Historical Alabama Maps and Gazetteers

Maps are necessary to genealogical research. They help us to locate landmarks, towns, cities, parishes, states, provinces, waterways and roads and streets. They also help us to determine when and where boundary changes might have taken place, and give us a visualization of the area we're researching in. For locating place names, a gazetteer is the best possible resource for any genealogist. Gazetteers are also sometimes called "place name dictionaries", and can help you to locate the area in which you need to conduct research. Below are links to the maps and gazetteers for research in Alabama.

Peabody GNIS Service – Alabama
http://peabody.research.yale.edu/cgi-bin/Query.GNIS?ST=Alabama

Color Landform Atlas – Alabama
http://fermi.jhuapl.edu/states/al_0.html

Alabama Department of Archives and History County Maps
http://www.archives.state.al.us/counties.html

1985 U.S. Atlas http://www.livgenmi.com/1895/AL/

Alabama Hometown Locator

http://alabama.hometownlocator.com/

Alabama Genealogical Records

<u>Birth, Death, Marriage and Divorce Records</u> – Birth, death, and marriage records are the most basic, yet most important records attached to your ancestor. They are generally referred to as vital records as they record vital life events. The reason for their importance is that they not only place your ancestor in a specific place at a definite time, but potentially connect the individual to other relatives. Below is a list of repositories where you can find Alabama vital records

Vital County Records on Microfilm at the Alabama Department of Archives and History (ADAH)
http://www.archives.alabama.gov/referenc/vital.html

FamilySearch - partial index of Births and Christenings from 1881-1930 you can search online.

FamilySearch https://familysearch.org/search/collection/1661470

Alabama Loose Records Index - database of names compiled and indexed from loose county court records filmed by the Genealogical Society of Utah in cooperation with the Alabama Department of Archives and History

Alabama Loose Records Index
http://lrp.algensoc.org/lrpw/loader2.html

Census Reports

Census records are among the most important genealogical documents for placing your ancestor in a particular place at a specific time. Like BDM records, they can also lead you to other ancestors, particularly those who were living under the authority of the head of household. Following are the best places to find Alabama census records.

Alabama Department of Archives and History – Census reports from 1820-1930

624 Washington Ave
Montgomery, AL, United States
Tel: +1 334-242-4435

Website: http://www.archives.alabama.gov/referenc/census.html

Census Finder – Alabama – Includes early Spanish census reports of the Mobile district from 1786, 1787, and 1789, as well as census records from 1810-1920

Website: http://www.censusfinder.com/alabama.htm

USGenWeb Census Project – Image database of census reports by county.

Website: http://www.rootsweb.ancestry.com/~census/states/alabama/

Alabama Church Records

Church and synagogue records are a valuable resource, especially for baptisms, marriages, and burials that took place before 1900. There are a few challenges to locating and accessing church records, such as the multitude of religious denominations that exist. Once found however, they can reveal information about your ancestor that other records do not. You will need to at least have an idea of your ancestor's religious denomination, and in most cases you will have to visit a brick and mortar establishment to view them. Below are links archives that maintain church records, as well as a few databases that can be viewed online.

The **LDS Family History Library**- Has a few Alabama church records, however most remain in the care of local churches

LDS Family History Library
https://familysearch.org/search/catalog/results#count=20&query=%2Bsubject_id%3A405785

Samford University Library - maintains an inventory of Baptist records but also possesses many different Alabama denominations in their collection. To access the records however, you will have to visit the University campus. You will find the address below.

Samford University
800 Lakeshore Drive
Birmingham, AL 35229

Samford University Library – http://library.samford.edu/

The **Houghton Memorial Library (Huntington College)** - maintains a wealth of genealogical resources including records of the Methodist church.

Huntingdon College
1500 E. Fairview Avenue
Montgomery, AL 36106-2148
Phone: (334) 833-4421
Fax: (334) 263-4465
E-mail:edidwell@huntingdon.edu

Houghton Memorial Library
http://libguides.huntingdon.edu/website

The **Presbyterian Historical Society** – national repository for holds archival records, books, and artifacts that document the history of the Presbyterian tradition in America. Collection includes documentation on church legal and administrative decisions; the First and Second Great Awakenings; religion and life in Colonial America; social justice issues; the New Republic; the American Revolution; missionary work among the Asians, Africans, and Native Americans; Westward expansion; the Civil War and Reconstruction; Civil Rights and other race issues; and ecumenical movements.

425 Lombard Street
Philadelphia, PA 19147
Phone: (215) 627-1852
Fax: (215) 627-0509

Presbyterian Historical Society http://www.history.pcusa.org/

The **Catholic Diocese of Birmingham** and the **Archdiocese of Mobile Archives**
– can be contacted to request records of the Catholic faith.

Diocese of Birmingham
2121 3rd Ave.
P.O. Box 12047
North Birmingham, AL 35202-2047
Phone: (205) 838-8322

Archdiocese of Mobile Archives
14 S. Franklin St.
Mobile, AL 36602
Phone: (251) 415-3850

Catholic Diocese of Birmingham : http://www.bhmdiocese.org/

Archdiocese of Mobile Archives
http://www.mobilearchdiocese.org/archives/archives.cfm?AOMDept
ID=21

Alabama Military Records

More than 40 million Americans have participated in some time of war service since America was colonized. The chance of finding your ancestor amongst those records is exceptionally high. Military records can even reveal individuals who never actually served, such as those who registered for the two World Wars but were never called to duty. Below are a number of links to websites and archives that hold a wealth of Alabama military records.

Alabama Civil War Roots – website hosting a number of links to a variety of Civil War records and histories that include; unit histories, cemetery records, enrollment forms, rosters, and military prison records.

Website: http://www.rootsweb.ancestry.com/~alcwroot/

Confederate States Navy Museum, Library and Research Institute – burial records and gravestone information of Confederate Navy and Marine veterans, including those buried in foreign countries.

Website: http://www.csnavy.org/

The Fold3 website hosts a database of **Alabama War of 1812 Records** that can be browsed online. The collection includes casualty reports, burial records, service records, and other documentation.

Alabama War of 1812 Records
http://www.fold3.com/browse.php#247|h5iT6dgqRLle5B31p

The **Alabama Department of Archives and History Military Records Collection** – contains records of the Revolutionary War, War of 1812, First and Second Creek Wars, Texas War for Independence, Mexican War, Civil War, Spanish American War, First and Second World Wars, Korean War, and the Vietnam War.

Alabama Department of Archives and History Military Records Collection http://www.archives.alabama.gov/referenc/military.html

Alabama Cemetery Records and Obituaries

As convenient as it is to search cemetery records online, keep in mind that there are a few disadvantages over visiting a cemetery in person. They are:

1. Tombstone information may not always be accurately transcribed
2. The arrangement of the graves in a cemetery can be crucial as family members are often buried next to each other or in the same grave. This arrangement is not always preserved in the alphabetical indexes that are found online.

With that information in mind, the following websites have databases that can be searched online.

Find a Grave – over 100 million grave records can be searched on this site. Search can be conducted by name, location, or cemetery name.

Website: http://www.findagrave.com/

Interment.net - A free online database containing cemetery records from thousands of cemeteries around the world. Consists of approximately 4 million cemetery records.

Website: http://www.interment.net/

Tombstone Transcription Project – A USGenWeb project, here you can browse cemetery transcriptions by state and county.

Website: http://www.usgwtombstones.org/

Billion Graves – as the name implies, you can search a billion records including headstone photos, transcriptions, cemetery records, and grave locations.

Website: http://billiongraves.com/pages/search/index.php#cemetery

US Department of Veterans Affairs Nationwide Gravesite Locator – includes information on veterans and their family members buried in veterans and military cemeteries having a government grave marker.

Website: http://gravelocator.cem.va.gov/

Daughters of the American Revolution Library – cemetery records and tombstone inscriptions from Alabama cemeteries.

Website: http://www.dar.org/library/

Alabama Obituaries

Obituaries can reveal a wealth about our ancestor and other relatives. You can search **Alabama Newspaper Obituaries Listings** from hundreds of Alabama newspapers online for free.

Alabama Newspaper Obituaries Listings

http://obituarieshelp.org/alabama_newspaper_obituaries.html

Alabama Wills and Probate Records

The documents found in a probate packet may include a complete inventory of a person's estate, newspaper entries, witness testimony, a copy of a will, list of debtors and creditors, names of executors or trustees, names of heirs. They can not only tell you about the ancestor you're currently researching, but lead to other ancestors. Most of these records must be accessed at a county court or clerk's office, but some can be found online as well.

The **Alabama Department of Revenue** provides the address and contact information of every county probate office in the state.

The **Family History Library** possesses microfilmed copies of probate records from the majority of counties in Alabama, usually from the date a county was created to the 1920s.

Alabama Department of Revenue
http://revenue.alabama.gov/licenses/authrity.cfm

Family History Library

https://familysearch.org/learn/wiki/en/Alabama,_County_Probate_R

ecords_(FamilySearch_Historical_Records)

Immigration and Naturalization Records

The naturalization process generated many types of records, including petitions, declarations of intention, and oaths of allegiance. Different records provide different details about the individual, such as age, ethnic background, country of birth, previous residences, current address, name of the ship sailed on, and date and port of arrival. Nationalization records are normally held at county level, but federal and state records were also generated. The best place to request naturalization records for Alabama is at the **National Archives Southeast Region (Atlanta).**

National Archives Southeast Region (Atlanta)
5780 Jonesboro Road
Morrow, Georgia 30260
Tel: 770-968-2100
Fax: 770-968-2547
EMail: atlanta.archives@nara.gov

Website: http://www.archives.gov/atlanta/

One of the biggest challenges facing family historians is locating information about immigrant ancestors. Discovering the name of your ancestor's original town, city, county, parish, or country of origin is an important goal. During the early 1700s, some Spanish and French families immigrated to Alabama's southern coastal area, but most settlers who arrived pre-statehood emigrated from the older southern states, especially Georgia and Carolina.

FamilySearch.org maintains an online index of **Passenger Arrivals, Atlantic and Gulf Ports, 1820-1874**, while the National Genealogical Society has a database of **Anglos and Anglo-Americans in Early Alabama.** The US National Archives has **Ships Passenger Lists** for immigrants arriving in the United States from overseas between the years 1820 and 1982.

Passenger Arrivals, Atlantic and Gulf Ports, 1820-1874
https://familysearch.org/search/collection/1921756

Anglos and Anglo-Americans in Early Alabama
http://www.ngsgenealogy.org/cs/references_for_researching

Ships Passenger Lists
http://www.archives.gov/research/immigration/

Alabama City Directories

City directories are similar to telephone directories in that they list the residents of a particular area. The difference though is what is important to genealogists, and that is they pre-date telephone directories. You can find an ancestor's information such as their street address, place of employment, occupation, or the name of their spouse. An excellent starting point for finding city directories is the **City Directories of the United States** website, where you can search alphabetical listing of directories for the entire state.

City Directories of the United States
http://www.uscitydirectories.com/al.htm

Missing Matriarchs – Resources for Researching Female Alabama Ancestors

Looking for female ancestors requires an adjustment of how we view traditional records sources. A woman's identity was often under that of her husband, and often individual records for them can be difficult to locate. The following resources are effective in locating female ancestors where traditional records may not reveal them.

Marriage and Divorce Records

1. County Courthouses
2. State Archives
3. University of South Alabama Archives
4. Alabama Department of Health

Civil War Pension Records

1. Alabama Department of Archives and History

Bibliographies

2. *City Belles: Images and Realities of the Lives of White Women in Antebellum Mobile*, by Harrier E. Amos
3. *Alabama Women: Roles and Rebels*, by Ann Boucher
4. *Marriages and Death Notices from Alabama Newspapers and Family records, 1819-1890*, Helen S. Foley
5. *A Collection of Biographies of Women Who made a Difference in Alabama*, by League of Women Voters of Alabama
6. *Partners in rebellion: Alabama Women in the civil War*, by H.E. Sterkx
7. *Stepping Out of the Shadows: Alabama Women 1819-1990*, by Montgomery: University of Alabama Press

Selected Resources for Women's History

Women's Army Corps Museum
Building 1077
Fort McClellan, Al. 36205-5000

W.S. Hoole Special Collections Library
University of Alabama
Po Box S
Tuscaloosa, AL. 35487

Common Alabama Surnames

The following surnames are among the most common in Alabama. The list is by no means exhaustive. If your surname doesn't appear in the list it doesn't mean that you have no Alabama connections, only that your surname may be less common.

Arner, Adams, Adamson, Aldridge, Allen, Amos, Arrington, Babcock, Bailey, Baker, Ballard, Barber, Barrow, Bassett, Beard, Bell, Black, Blackmon, Boswell, Boyd, Bright, Brown, Brumbelow, Bryan, Bryant, Burdett, Burson, Bush, Canady, Cannon, Carson, Carter, Chisholm, Clifton, Clinton, Cohen, Coker, Cole, Conoway, Cotton, Crabtree, Crosby, Crumby, Cullars, Davis, Denham, Dozier, Duke, Elkins, Emory, Eters, Evans, Factor, Farris, Farrow, Faust, Flanigan, Flannegan, Flowers, Fortune, Freeman, Fuller, Garner, Gibson, Graves, Greer, Green, Griffith, Griggs, Hadaway, Hall, Hardy, Harris, Haynie, Holley, Horne, Hughey, Hurston, Hussey, Johnson, Jones, Jordan, Kelly, King, Kirk, Kittley, Knight, Knowles, Lambert, Lancaster, Lashley, Lecroy, Levey, Lewis, Lucas, Mackey, Martin, Mason, Mayo, Mcinish, Miller, Mitchell, Moncrief, Morris, Nail, Northcut, Pate, Pearson, Philips, Pike, Pope, Powell, Prather, Rabun, Ray, Reese, Rice, Robertson, Robinson, Rockwell, Rogers, Royster, Rushing, Shearer, Sims, Smith, Strickland, Sullivan, Taylor, Thaxton, Thomas, Thrower, Tucker, Vestal, Waldrop, Walker, Watkins, Whitehead, Whittington, Williams, Williamson, Willingham, Wilson, Wimberley, Wisener, Worthy, Wright, Yates,